MAY 1 7 2010 DATE DUE		
JUL 1 7 2010		
OCT 0 9 2010		
MAR 1 1 2011		
DISCARDED BY URBANA FREE LI		

A MOUTH IN CALIFORNIA

Graham Foust

FLOOD EDITIONS

A Mouth in California

2009

4/10

15.00

ISBN 978-0-9819520-1-7

Design and composition by Quemadura
Cover painting: Brian Calvin, *Killer*,
2006, courtesy of the artist and
Anton Kern Gallery, New York
Printed on acid-free, recycled paper
in the United States of America

This book was made possible
in part through a grant from
the Illinois Arts Council

FIRST EDITION

TO PETER KLAPPERT AND SUSAN HOWE

BUDGE What amazes me is this. Your body is falling apart
but your voice is strong.

GRASS My voice isn't part of my body. It's what comes out
of my body when I speak. It's the air which by some miracle
we are able to shape into the sounds we wish to make.

BUDGE A lovely insight. See? You're capable.

GRASS Some people are genetically coded for greatness.
Some are foreign-born. Some go to the racetrack every day,
take the special train, study the form. What an interesting
thing a horse is, when you think of it.

BUDGE Who was the first person who decided to get on top
of one?

GRASS Exactly.

BUDGE Scary.

GRASS Right.

[DON DELILLO, *The Day Room*]

A MOUTH IN CALIFORNIA

THE SUN ALSO FIZZLES

What's this place, between
geography and evening? The sun
also bludgeons; a car has three wheels;
and what's the wrong way to break
that brick of truth back into music?

Money belongs together. I'm right
where I wanted to leave me. Rain
belongs together. At mirror,
I've neither me believed.

I've come covered in arena dust,
my mouth a sleeve's end,
meatless. I've come somewhat up,
and I'm here to lick
the static from the ground.

Twice, I've been evidence of,
if anything, my breathing.
Not particular, I've pissed against
a cage, pretending wind.

Swallowed whole, a songbird might
could claw back through the hawk—
or so I've thought.
The choosing of a word
might be its use, the only poem.

TO THE WRITER

Another cloud spun to nothing, one
of nature's more manageable kills.
Another borderline-meaningless morning save
for everything. You claim you kissed
a certain picture with such patience
you became it. So who hasn't?
You're of one long weary trouble;
you wear your hard mind on your hand.

Thus, your dumb touch, your clunky
fuss, your little millions. Your stomach
newly stuffed with amputations. Quiet
and furious dots of distant rooms—rooms,
I would add, through which you'll never move
or sleep—begin to mean. In one of them,
humor, collapsed in a painful curl, an odd
head at the back of its throat. It's what's to bleed about.

REAL JOB

To trip the forced majestic.

To then almost fall ahead.

To make a darkness.

To then light up the fortunate dead.

To burst into question, into voiced-over nerves.

To then groan a few where-was-I's in a morning's weird gold.

To think to leave a place forever, wherever you are.

To then head back through the gate, your basic yard.

To lay off the day's controls and keep your suit on like a scar.

To then improvise restraint behind an open, broken door.

To say, "The dream was in me like a bone."

To then mean it.

To listen for the pill to never come.

To then sleep.

To sleep the half-sleep of the flammable, whoever they are.

To then not regret—so be it—your alarm.

To feel that every possible shape's been made.

To then crush a cup of water.

To crush another cup of water.

To then work the human room.

POEM WITH MANIFEST DESTINY

Comedic wagons, tasty
venom. A mouth on
every bird. To planet snaps
the day sky's blank
vaccine, the moviest
thing. Until we make
a note of it, meat
is motion, a crush
of exercise. We get
our tongues pierced just
for the lisps, the faint clucks.
A document's the dust
between belief and any cracked-
but-working implement.

LYRIC POETRY AFTER V-E DAY

These were a dream's prerequisites:
war and then war and then
war and then war and then insects
testing for sweetness. Electric
bulbs! Early in marriage, he'd switched
them off, saved money. She'd wanted
a bright and more welcoming home.
Late in same, she'd dimmed them
for what someone else called *ambiance*.
He'd wanted light, God damn it,
so as to see. I think they're dead now
or something. I'm only writing this.
Pretend and two dimensional, I am
and so have always been barbaric.

FOR PETER RAMOS

POEM BESIDE ITSELF

Where in the capsized animal
am I. Came to to find you tapping at
a padlock with a hammer.

You there, there in the ash there,
screwed to the past like a kiss.

You've never had to kill me.
You have nowhere but the air.
These birds are so clearly not
words, and they've been everywhere.
Their eyes are here, always, and time.

Cut to ground. Cue tremors.
Cue pedestrians and vowels.
Cue the landscape brandishing
itself with lazy malice.

Cue a usual night with planets burning
out at one another. Cue toys in their aisles—
I said cue tremors!—and queer every relevant dream.

Sky again. A flower or
a cloud exactly like it.
Either clean of any idea.

The by-heart bags of music
in this body are collapsing.
This carved little mind I've been
smashing around in, thinking
around with, is flashing, not
with plastic or with shadow
or with damaging winds
or laughter, but with plans—
I plan at you; I play unsanitary;
I point and I pull at your eyes.

I say, "Duck duck chain"
and I say, "Chain chain goose"
and should you feel a person tearing at
your hands, delay the why.

Tongues for which the crowd slows: shed 'em.
What is what is made of sleep from.
Numb with light, polite, and wealth-
mouthing, I pose with my bones.

You've never had to kill me.
What takes place in me stays there.

These words are so clearly not
birds—they'll never be anywhere.
Show me how God has a face.

Keep talking while I tend to the lines on your face.
Keep talking while I touch your face
and keep talking through your face
and throw your face through your face.

POEM WITH CONCUSSION

Can't think, but there's wind—
and in the wind another clarified
field and people sprinting to fix things.
Someone's clothes are in the road;
the snows of Brueghel
and after-market video coat the road.
I see a thick flash of paint, a stiff
light and I'm blind as a bell.

The mind's the eye we cry
the body through. Says here
the rub's a bruise. I want all the way—
the only way I know I don't know how—
into the house. I want the deep glare
I've just unveiled to not tear
my air away. I want to turn up in
my head to not be hit.

FROST AT MIDNIGHT

Little cinders are apt to be empty.
The cold's a bond, and it's also the cold.
I've slashed my finger on a toy, postponed
the peach-toned plastic strap across the cut.
My blood's come up for a visit—now what?
And what if I said that the woodstove reeks
of that old lover of yours who punched me?
Brick to my ears, the winter night beyond
gone, I'd get to nothing but to feeling
like I just had to put some flesh between
these teeth before the planet shut, that's what.
Chunks of old smoke, my ideas disappear.
The backs of my cheeks are raw with habit.
"Think," says every hole in me. You know that.

POEM WITH FEAR,

AS HALF-AWAKENED

See, I might return—the car's gassed,
the map flat and likely accurate—
to where I'm clear to me to you.
This'd be autumn, let's say, like late
October, mid-November. By then
the road'll be choked with leaves
and other ruins, the trees with wind
and smoke and dark (or not).
I'll make records of these facts,
these other shores. My song'll be a nail
and yours, a mouthful of mirror.
Seconds before we sing, I'll be reading
that wading pool's dismal little slaps
to mean trouble. You'll punch an animal,
any animal; I'll touch a small bell;
the moon'll turn everything lurid.
But what good is said moon
if neither song'll fit the room?
Come with platitudes, love,
come whatever doesn't move.

AFTER TAXES

We're more distant in the red, more ugly.
I don't know, but I've been told it's a fear:
There are things less important than money.

It's a little like watching paint not dry
Or like a bomb didn't go off in here.
We're more boring in the dark, less ugly.

We watch the moon get up on its gurney.
We try to pretend it's a chandelier.
There are things less important than money.

Come dawn, we're the Polaroid of mercy,
Our stomachs left unpuckered by our spears.
Reinvented by sleep, we're still ugly.

Stapled to the promise of the daily
Rage to purchase, our cause is close to clear.
There are things less important than money.

Our heads are talking over us, honey,
And there was never not a fiscal year.
We're timeless in the red, beyond ugly.
There are things less important than money.

FROM A MOUTH IN CALIFORNIA

Shorts and a t-shirt. Not even
nothing's bitten into you.
And to think they call this lack
of shrapnel "fall."
Last night was all corners; this morning
sports a fumbled-up glow.
With your marrowy kilter, you've
believed into this weather, grown
to hate some certain turns and times
of day, but you're mostly okay:
a more plausible me, a less
unthinkable pile of holes.

Watch the world and it'll crack.
You'll see star dirt, sure, but let the sun
not be a lesson. There's a bruise at the end
of the light still hurts from way back.
There's this disease runs from "quit-
to-keep-staying" to "pressed-
for-safekeeping" and yes,

you can recycle it.

The people bells are different from
the God bells, but how?

The hell's a ghost before it gets to us?

You are only not thinking out loud now.

POEM TO REALISM

That you're real enough's
the trouble. That's
the chore here, the chore
of enchantment.

Real enough erupts
from too little, too much.
The wall's yours. You make
the subject stay the same.

WE ARRIVE AS IF AT A

PICTURE, PINCHED

into a syntax we grope for and map.

Second thought, next thought: snow—
just do, just don't. And the dark's parts
replace themselves; the papers tell us
where to put our names. The world
will trade us, and trust's, oh, I don't know,
a stunt, irreverence tedious. Enormity's
adorable, but only the broken breathe.
My disappointment in the poem's voicey
noise is too easy. I push throat after throat
through the bones of my ears. There's
no method, no code in the grass-deep grid.
And just now our son stands on a dead (I
think) baby bird, and he touches that
cracked ceramic rabbit as if it's alive.

FOR AMY HEZEL

POEM WITH RULES AND LAWS

You don't lust
for what you
want. You lust
for what you
can get. I'll
carve you your
hankered-for
chemical
oath. I'll show
you the badge
in my mouth.

POEM WITH GROWNUP

For want
of Percocet, militant
hurt. For real
I bitched and withered:
none of the water
was mine. Dirt
out a window. Me
in a window, faint
of head and loud
of mind. Daylight
on muscle, that
been-gnawed-at
quality. Dirt
on a window.
I'd've loved it
had I cried.

POEM WITH SIDE EFFECT

Every recollection—from the smallest, most in-
significant jangle of trash to watching
someone care for machines to fan-blade
shadows to showers of blood—begins
as a secret. (That's the truth, and of course
I can't prove it; I think I mean what I don't
want to say.) But why's the dull tangle of denial
half of life? Lying's lonely—to lie
alone at least is good. And I'm over here, keeping
split, requiring assembly. Forget weeping.
Get silent. My lack of desire says hi.

MY GRAHAM FOUST

Gone's his imposter, and gone's
his gawky cross. Gone's
his tweaked legacy's hit list—hooray!—
and gone's his waste of song.

Gone's his civilized wrist. Gone's
his long-exploded gut. Gone's his cruel joy,
his humbling drunk, his good tired.
Gone's his one and every clod of common sense.

Gone's the water from under his mumble.
Gone's his mumble from up in the room.
Yet to go are his books and his bloodless clothes
and shoes. Gone's his broken oven and its beef.

Gone's his wet secret. Gone's
his pillar and what it let fall.
Gone's his excellent source of nothing,
his kick-ass pettiness, his premium harm.

Gone's the bite of you he spit. Gone's
his vague sense of what's to be done.
Gone's the dream that likely scraped at him
for more and more and more and gone's his walk.

Gone's his crass commiseration. Gone's
his shack of gauze and ice. Gone's
his tiny fountain. And gone
is his glutinous light.

Gone's his want-to-need basis. Gone's his happy
plastic stain. Gone's his glass wolf, his lazy sperm,
his pack of exactness. Gone's his played-through lack
of played-through games of pain.

Gone's his fleshy shovel.
Gone's his ticket; gone's his train.
Gone's the friend who stepped away
and almost saved him. Gone's the blame.

Gone's his sister. Gone's his doctor.
Gone's his transom. Gone's his view.
He's nobody's autobiography.
Whose are you.

THEIR EARLY TWENTIES

Full of noise and lust, they fled
the city for the shore. It was four
in the upcoming morning. Everyone
slobbered; somebody drove.
Another thirst begun, they had their beer
in cans in bags; their hands, their feet
in frigid sand; their eardrums—make that
their headaches—sewn with ocean.
They'd never seen a moon so willful,
so scissory, never heard the dark water
rearrange so clumsily. Crowded future,
dingy beach. They scratched the air;
they burned and buried things.
They were the fruit they couldn't reach.

MISSISSIPPI BACKWARDS

Give me reasons not to be
oblivion, irony. How am I
for time, retarded artifacts,
old money? The grandiose
grows tiresome. A credible rain
re-ups the grass. And so it goes:
I dig me my imaginary trench—
the major forests filling in; the flashing
oceans pushing back; my memories wrapped
with scratches, thumbs for crutches, plus
blisters galore. I buy whatever sense there is.
I'm only stories, old or other, toward which
I'm insisted. And when I'm dead I'm just
the dark's prank. When I'm gone
I'll be the song I wrote to get me back
to ash. I first heard loss in a place
with every weather—as the dullest
possible bombast, a record I forgot
I'd never owned—and then I went home.
But here, there, in that trench that I mentioned,

my insufficient fiction, there's an all-new boredom:
loud / quiet / loud / quiet quite without trying,
a boredom of cathedral proportion. Full-on folk,
I've just made up, made over everything.
I'm in and out of pieces.
My tongue's at
disaster's ear.

MORALITY AND

TEMPORAL SEQUENCE

Funny. Night after, you've trouble
sleeping without your glasses. Every
noise upends you—the click of the tooth-
like lightswitch; the window blinds gnashing
in the small, hot wind; a fan churning fast
and close. And you fumble for the frames
in the rickety dark. You see clearly
for an hour, and then you dream. Come
dawn, you're awake, make coffee. You burn
your lips on the first few sips, and then
you pour the rest away. You flip coins.
And when the sun gets its whole way up,
you halfway worry: where's that chunk of skull
while the surgeon's inside? This was
our house, you say inside yourself. Here
are untold filthy jokes, terrific
ghosts in every crevice. Pull them near.

THE CALL

Windows. Where
do you not want
to go today.

You. You.
You. Y O U.
Regret's not letting up.

Reason wants
a lift from where
you left it.

SCRAPS AFTER REVERDY

Near embers, tears.

Still warm here.

Where's that hand.

◆

A sky crawls
across itself

and sinks to float
its clouds.

A wave gives
up. A field continues.

◆

You could stay. We could sleep.
I could drop things, die.

◆

The wind's no slave.
Flames worship it.

♦

Loose shingles are perfect for poems.

POEM FOR JACK SPICER

The more I pull it all to pixels
the more to sleep the radio goes,
right? And to be dead would be to be
modern? At the at-once bustling and
dismally hushed airport, goodbye'll
just congeal into a condition;
the jets, they've got that rained-around look.
Not unbreakable, hand in imagined
hand, I used to insist on fading
stations, fact's outskirts, a back to the void.
Paper for water and water for air,
I'd think for words and tremble numbers,
remember? Wasn't that where I lived?
This ocean, I just assumed it would
look bigger. Its poem's shape's itself,
and its waves come off as contagious.
Kick the curtain. Kick the rain. Space, too,
will tear a way through us. Later, though,
there could be peace like a flaccid hex,
one weepable question in the blooms.

I might then shred said sad question, try
to take up its traces, remake it,
but I've got no blueprints, not a tool;
the shed's done dog-eared into the dirt.
When no one knows my name, I look half
different under my silvery Bank
of America gift umbrella,
and unlike other thrashed visuals,
the sun still crams light into the world.
I mean to be in that light and in
the world in the way that I meant to
show up in the picture just snapped by
some stranger in the middle distance.
It's not a thicket if I can't get
me and whoever else into it—
let's call what I'm *on* a moon of hurt.
We're all limited by the plumb line,
that imperative that collapses
in the directions of egg and ash.
There should be more works of art like those
on which I wrote no dissertation.
The animal empire just scratches.
I am trying to make my skin run.

THE ONLY POEM

This is not a machine.
It does not kill fascists.
You're pretending to see the light.

Winter. Some river,
its claws of water stalled.
You walk across, crossing this, it.

You trust ice, the thermometer,
and riotous loss. Even in danger
you're a writer, liar.

SECRET RERUN

Even unthreatened, you're
a goner, singer. Say this
and your face goes under.
We're of the same dark ages,
same flashes, but my mouth
is more a cause-effect flower.
There's a room (Hello!) full
of everything we've ever
outgrown, and not a bit of it
is money. The creatures there
were killed for so much less
than their obvious weakness.
The barely-dreamt-of alarm's
the more frequent alarm.
I make me explain: a flashing
machine's shine's missing.
The screen's a slice of lecture, dire
with color. Calculable (Got it!)
and radiant cuts, that's

the policy. The world
was always yours, you.
The dead are fine. The dead
are fine. The dead are fine.

POEM FOR ROBERT CREELEY

The darker sphere of day
that holds the night up barely
watches me. The chimes can't
touch each other now
so music rests. (The wind
is elsewhere.) And life, no matter
whose or how real—and matter:
expensive, relative, irrelevant—
all of it suffices precisely,
slightly. All of this
undoes just what you're not.

LOS ANGELES

Loss of faith is

growth is faith. The only critique
of paradise is paradise.

Be there drinking,

our shared throat shallow in all
direction, then nothing.

In this particular

version of everywhere, a movie equal to
and other than

our memory disappears.

We imagine *wanting*. And here, our wanting
is at its most tangible. The movie turns

into itself. What not for?

POEM WITH TELEVISION

But first another picture of the world.

◆

I thought I saw you in
the mirror through the window.

You do
remember don't you.

Absence of evidence isn't an answer.

◆

I thought you saw me through
the window in the mirror.

You don't
remember do you.

Evidence of absence isn't an answer.

◆

What part of
"What part of no

don't you understand?"
don't you understand

on one more American-
money ugly morning,

busy-intersection
skittish in a bed?

◆

Greased, it would seem, what I call
what I used to call
belief slides through me.

Is it just me, or am I alone?

At the end of the night, night.
Night again. Another night.
Or do I say that it's *still* night, night
continued? Part of me—not quite
my working face—would just love to.
And months approach like stones.

Wilted to official, I might keep
here like a leaf. Might eat
my prayer. Might say
to feign astonishment
and where. The absolute
bleeds between these places,
half inflated. What I get's
a nick of space, these reams of paper.

Today's blazing in a place
we've only heard of.
And you say, "Here's theory
in/or your eye, beholder."

◆

That we're free enough's
the trouble. We're fucked
for now, finally. Mock-ups
are made, already hated,
wasteful. We think
we see the blast
and then we watch the blast
relax. We learn the chains.

◆

Today's blazing is a place
we've only heard of.
And you say, "The laugh in grief's way
is grief's way with us."

WAKING VERY LATE

ON HALLOWEEN

Hey I'm just grinding
some iris here, destroying
old feeling, when who
demands my aid?

Sung up from the far-
off interest of sleep,
I get bug-sudden music,
a pain-blue light.

Shadows cross, cross
and uncross,
as absent
as what makes them.

Night reads today to me.
A little orange kid
veering through the street
screams screams.

THAT PANIC

When your head
was as busy
and indiscriminate
as flames, you kept
on sucking.

Given thinking's
blown gland, another
breath was at least—
or was at best—
not nothing.

AFTER MARGARET ATWOOD

I fit into you
like a peg into a hole

a tent peg
a donut hole

POEM WITH FEELINGS

Thoughts of them, thought
or not,
are mostly that.

There's always
been a pointlessness.
Rejoice.

POEM WITH PREMONITIONS

Stirred into itself, its ideas
for dreams in place, the body—
impersonal, perfect—is barely a sign.

Yours does blood to return
to meanwhile. Mine
does bright nightmare with hand.

Afraid of different deaths,
we wake
in equally sleep-pocked beds.

A HEAP OF LANGUAGE

I wash the knives and wipe
the table. You come from the ocean
and dry yourself. Inside us, apologies inch
their way around. Most of what we say will hardly matter.

HAPPENING PASTORAL

And fell awake or like it. And did parade
the bleaching field. (And the grass there was action.
And the soil more real than you'd imagined.)
And looked for something growing, something
not okay to break. And got busy. And so tractored out
the ground. And now your tongue, so abused by its making
that it no longer means much, crawls.
And now there's only looking and the field.
And the field. And the relatively small-
scale killings in the field. And gray, gray
and not-gray, gray and maybe-gray, gray
and gray. And you sink, bad swimmer, your skin-side
up, your surrogate face put first to endless nettles.
And from intricate fruit to simple bone, you'll say
you love your body. And your drastic need to be.

MASTURBATORY

And so "self-love" may be taken two ways.

JONATHAN EDWARDS

Like a kind of rain, I
cling in traces, withstanding
unequally real occasions:
a guard dog gnashes at
the sky is rapture's opposite;
the wind thumbs through
a flag thumbs through a flag.
And just above my throat, that
laughing capital of me, sits
a succulent ditch, blows a set
of less-acceptable breezes:
here goes—. What this is
is arousal's residue, the hands
as hands and someone else.

SQUEEZE OUT THE LIGHTS

Monday, Tuesday, forever. In one
memory and in the other, I'm paid
to stray from places where I've tried
to count quietly. I'm paid to not
break open in the dark. Clouds
already, the cold glass as always;
an hour with all the thrill of a faded
stain, an average love. I've just
been hovering over my blood—
and that's something—but grief
is neither thought nor grief
enough; the facts aren't working.
No one walks into a room, and so
I go out through my mouth. No
one walks into a room. And so on.
These palaces still still palaces.

FOUR POEMS CALLED

"THE POEM"

trails me not unlike a savior, an assailant.

◆

: think to listen at me break it.

◆

works to a skin—and then back—from within.

◆

is too very mute to not be hindered.

IF I DID IT; OR, THE

MAXIMUS POEM

If knowing meant a little something here,
you'd know to shiver or burn
without me. Whatever. Live forever
and you'll kill. Once around wind, its very
antonym, a brain will chase or hide.
And so I run from and hunt for me,
asleep above myself, below clouds
the size of birds and bundles of whips
and the operative leaves. I don't love you
like I love you; I don't drag out the too-
late light like I love you: cold contour
after contour in a full, dark room; the calm
hauling of the gravity of not-unconscious lists.

I'm just homesick with similarity, overfamiliar
having been here endlessly already.
Next day, I'm sore from comfort. The sky
is thick as a tool. I'm best at the last thing

we need, believe me—I'll hold you until I'm alone.
I've forgotten who taught me how to swim
but I remember how to swim and I'm an American.
And I forget about my blood, about
how blood's not trace enough. About
the required machines and mirages, these keys
in my fist. No pictures of this exist.
But if one turns up, you'll come get me, okay?
And then I'll break it like you own a hundred more.

POEM FOR EZRA POUND

AND JOHNNY KNOXVILLE

Back away from
and so into you—

your every bone
a blaze—

as if deep
dim human ruin came

to news you'd want
to freeze.

SO MOVED

I, duly finite, pass from animal to remnant.

If for anything, the meat of me votes to get away.

All day, reflections from beside-the-point life click by me.

Last one crossed from the list in the sand's the youngest ghost.

OUTBOX

You refuse to spell correctly the famous
name of the famous town in which
you'll lie to someone other than me tonight.
"And he," you write, "is very dying."

But get this: a glossy sun in that
obscenely slow gamut the sky.
Now get in love.
I'd so like to burn down your hands.

Heartbreak thrashes the hush, a mouth
of thought—I freak back out.
To space's constant swallow comes
a small unslaughter: a song
for once, a sliver. Be let go.

SAVE AS SAVE THE

LAST DANCE FOR ME

You are cordially invited to read something
else, and like a word I lean to please,
pieces: there's a wet log moaning
in the fire. I live, then, biographically:
I live a way of living, or—more correctly—
I live ways of living; I live plural-biographically,
torn up between Kant and some dove.
Wire-hearted here—on this, my first day online
since the rumor died—I drink into a box of pink light.
Nobody help me. I'm someone I'm
almost not. With a look, I could break your bright
teeth, you gulping hero. The rest is research—
big minute, big minute, more later—
the old thought jerking like a flame.

AFTER MARY HEILMANN

very cold. My small
and spastic last
kiss was like making
a noise to make sure
I was there.

Your quiet
mouth was only
space—a kiss
reversed and kept
inside to bite.

POEM WITH PREMATURE

EJACULATION

Now is a hinge and again
and again and
feels infinite and isn't.

Its fire is dull, real.
I should know—
I'm a stack of its ashes.

I think milk. I hang back in explicit
grass, two, three.
And the skies are not cloudy all day.

WHAT WOKE ME

Not the minor
quake but

the dissonant
taste

of a paint
chip.

POEM WITH LIFESTYLE

I want to be beaten

within an inch of my likeness
and/or my liking it. Accuracy
only counts on runways
and in fakery. You are only
here to leave me alone.

I plummet home.

I am all night working on
a lie but suck it back.
I'm hours without water,
talk, or child.

The road? Can't see it:

no moon—but does it hum!
And this is my mouth to come
right on out and say so.
And this is my mouth to go
erasing loudly down.

SELF-PORTRAIT

IN SUPERTARGET

Scrutinized by scores of raging
white fluorescent lights, you've not
been watching you. But like
a potter working clay to make
a bottle that may one day keep
your teeth, you bet you yank
and pinch and push and smile.
Abrupt, dumb—your whole
lifetime, finally—your song
decides, as though crushed,
to say nothing. You tongue
imagined money up the aisle.

TODAY THE BARRICADES

are only turnstiles. And it's true it's such
that just enough God is too much,
that moods are instantly memory,
theory. Today's day's needs
've made a knife of me.
In the last of our collapse, I'll hurt early
and in color. I'll cut miles of tasteless
shapes from each citizen's hands.

Cold flags whip the empty.
They don't give trophies for frenzy,
do they? On a different day,
a different *kind* of day,
I'd stick me to some blessed
and irrelevant stand.

NUANCES OF A THEME

BY STEVENS; OR, WHY

I LOVE COUNTRY MUSIC

These sounds are long in the living of the ear.
The honky-tonk out of the somnolent grasses
Is a memorizing, a trying out, to keep.

◆

What I wanted to say—the wind ripping up
and into everywhere—was "Don't say nothing."
This was not allowed.

What I said was "Don't say anything."
This, too, was not allowed—the wind, again,
ripping up and into everywhere.

The truth, I knew it: breath and heaven—one thing.
A thing for shrieky talk and fearless error.
A thing about to happen to anyone.

ON FORM FOR HAGGARD

your "Long Black
Limousine"

depends so much
upon

mistakes: a missed
turn

"the curve nobody
seen"

POEM NOT TO MOMMY

OR THE OCEAN

I cross the clear
alarm, the nonsense of not
being stared at, and I sleep.
I go again, not crying,
to the dream in which I cry
to find meticulous flutters of blades
and blades of clouds, a bent
badge of moon as daylight's eyelet—
you are there.

I'm here and you
were here and I was there—
I want to be where?
Beware: I'll try
to make a number
to remember. I'll do
the wrong thing in the life
I don't see, the clean
hell of revery I can't leave.

DIFFICULTY SWALLOWING

A pause
arose.
Nothing on
paper.

Have it
and have at it.
Work. Earn. Hurt.

You can't spell *taxidermist*
without *Marxist*.

◆

You are
who you sleep with.
Borrow zero. Bother
no one.

You are
who you think
you are.

Unwelcome
home.

PERHAPS I HAVE NOT MENTIONED

THAT I AM DISMANTLING A HOUSE

I am dismantling a house.

You are not thinking this in a way
very different from the way
I am not thinking this. You're

hallucinatory, which is to say
real until proven otherwise.
Now hide your cuts:
the culture's coming.
The fact of things happening

elsewhere and to others —
a fact with which we're rapt
but rarely smashed —
is on its way back.
Nothing. Nothing. Knock knock knock.
Now name another other world
refuses us pummeling.

POEM AT HOME

Everything, Earth, compares to you.
Everything in you seems aimed at me.
And now I know what these are for—

that is to say, that ladder and the fear
that I put it here, had it put here,
what have you.

Some days, you fake it
to me, flower out. Your animals
are not so unspecific.

A horse is a horse of course
of course. And then
there's that hornet at my door.

Many of the poems in this book borrow language from other sources. My thanks—and, if necessary, my apologies—to those people whose work has proved useful to me.

Thanks also to the editors of the following publications in which earlier versions of these poems first appeared: *The Alembic, Caffeine Destiny, Colorado Review, Conjunctions, The Cultural Society, Crowd, Denver Quarterly, Eucalyptus, Free Verse, The Laurel Review, Naked Punch, The Nation, Konundrum Engine Literary Review, New Ohio Review, Parthenon West Review, Ping Pong, Practice: New Writing + Art, A Public Space, Rust Buckle, Shampoo, Third Coast,* and *Typo.*

Thanks to Gordon Hadfield and Sasha Steensen, who published several of these poems in *Some Kinds of Poems,* a limited-edition chapbook from Bonfire Press.

Lastly, thanks to this book's first readers: Lily Brown, Logan Esdale, and Asa Muir-Harmony.

Graham Foust is the author of three previous books of poetry, including *Necessary Stranger* (Flood Editions, 2007). He lives in Oakland and teaches at Saint Mary's College of California.